1. Metals and non-metals

Interesting elements

There are 92 elements found naturally on Earth. An element is made up from only one type of atom. These atoms are Nature's building blocks.

Here's Tungsten – a real bright spark and strong too!

Tungsten glows white hot inside light bulbs

Here's Gold. Gold is very expensive and a rather attractive atom.

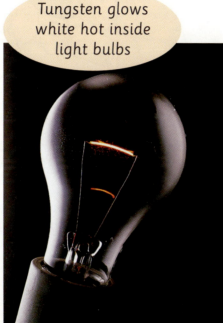

My little friend Hydrogen – the lightest of all of us.

The USA stores its gold in Fort Knox.

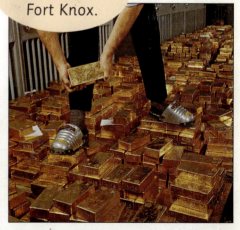

Hydrogen was used in airships because it is so light. However, disasters like this in 1937 soon stopped this use of the gas. Hydrogen is too reactive with the oxygen in the air to be used safely.

Q1 What is an element?

Q2 How many elements are found naturally on Earth?

Q3 Name the four elements on this page. List another four of your own. The next few pages might help you.

1. Metals and non-metals

Sorting out the elements: the Periodic Table

By 1800 scientists had started trying to sort out the elements. They had a difficult job. Many elements had not yet been discovered. They also thought that some things were elements that were really compounds.

In 1869, a Russian scientist called Dmitri Mendeleev solved the problem. He put the elements in order of mass, lining up similar elements in columns. He called this the **Periodic Table**. The columns are called **groups**.

These groups are like families of elements. The elements in a group are alike in many ways. If you know something about one element, you know a little about all the others in the same group. This made chemistry a lot easier!

▲ Sorting out the elements was like doing a jigsaw. Unfortunately, the scientists did not have a picture to guide them. They had some pieces missing. Other pieces did not even belong in the jigsaw.

The Periodic Table

1	2	Groups									3	4	5	6	7	8
					H											He
Li	Be										B	C	N	O	F	Ne
Na	Mg										Al	Si	P	S	Cl	Ar
K	Ca	Sc	Ti	V	Cr	Mn	Fe	Co	Ni	Cu	Zn	Ga	Ge	As	Se	Br	Kr
Rb	Sr	Y	Zr	Nb	Mo	Tc	Ru	Rh	Pd	Ag	Cd	In	Sn	Sb	Te	I	Xe
Cs	Ba	La	Hf	Ta	W	Re	Os	Ir	Pt	Au	Hg	Tl	Pb	Bi	Po	At	Rn

Q1 Why did scientists find it a hard job to sort out the elements at first?

Q2 How many groups are there in the Periodic Table?

Q3 Why are the groups important to scientists?

Q4 Which of the following elements is the odd one out? Say why.
Li (lithium), Na (sodium), Mg (magnesium), K (potassium), Rb (rubidium) and Cs (caesium).
(Hint: look at the Periodic Table)

Extension exercise 1 can be used now.

1. Metals and non-metals

Metal elements

More than three-quarters of the elements in the Periodic Table are metals. These metals have some very useful properties.

Metals are good **conductors of electricity**.

▲ Copper is used for electrical wiring.

Metals are good **conductors of heat**.

▲ Pans are often made of aluminium.

Metals are **malleable**. They can be hammered or stamped into shapes.

▲ The body of this car is stamped out of a sheet of steel. Steel is made up mainly from the element, iron.

Metals are **ductile**. They can be drawn out into wires.

▲ These guitar strings are made out of steel.

Metals make a **ringing sound** when hit.

▲ Big Ben is the name of the bell in the Houses of Parliament.

Metals are usually **strong** and **dense**.

▲ This bar has over 250 kg on either end, but it won't snap!

Metals are **shiny**.

▲ Headlights use metal reflectors to shine the light in the right direction.

Q1 Which metal is used for electrical wiring?

Q2 Which metal is often used to make pans?

Q3 Which metal is used to make steel?

Q4 What do these words mean:
a malleable
b ductile?

1. Metals and non-metals

Heating metals

Metals also have other useful properties. In this experiment you can try to melt some metals.

Apparatus
- iron ■ copper ■ nickel
- tongs ■ Bunsen burner
- heat-proof mat

Safety note: Wear eye protection when heating things.

A Hold the end of an iron nail in a pair of tongs. Heat the other end as strongly as you can. With the air hole open, the hottest part of the flame is at the tip of the blue cone.

B When there is no further change, let the iron cool down on your heat-proof mat.

C Repeat steps **A** and **B** with thick pieces of nickel and copper wire.

Q1 What happens when each metal is heated?

Q2 Do metals have high or low melting points?

Q3 Give two uses of metals where a high melting point is important.

Melting metals

It takes a lot of energy to melt most metals. For example, gold melts at 1064°C.

▲ Molten gold is poured into a mould to make rings.

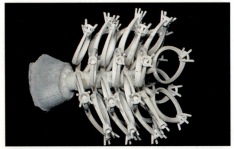

▲ Here are the rings.

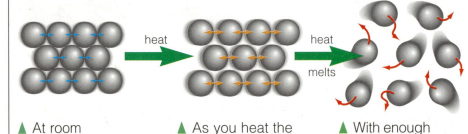

▲ At room temperature, the atoms in a metal vibrate (just like those in any solid).

▲ As you heat the atoms, they vibrate more and more quickly. (The metal expands.)

▲ With enough energy, the solid melts. It turns into a liquid. The atoms break free from each other. They can now move around.

Q4 What happens to the atoms in a metal as you heat it up above its melting point?

Q5 Do most metals have strong or weak forces between their atoms? Give a reason for your answer.

1. Metals and non-metals

Non-metals: solids

The opposite of a metal is a **non-metal**. There are only about 20 non-metal elements. Here are some of the **solid** non-metals.

▲ Sulphur is a yellow solid. It is found under the ground. Most of it is used to make sulphuric acid.

▲ White phosphorus is very dangerous. It reacts so easily with the oxygen in the air that it bursts into flames without heating. It must be stored in a jar filled with water.

Carbon is an interesting non-metal. It has two different forms: graphite and diamond. Graphite is the only non-metal that conducts electricity. It is a soft, flaky solid. Carbon atoms from graphite are left behind on your paper every time you use your pencil. Yet diamond is very different. It is one of the hardest substances in the world.

▼ The end of this drill is lined with diamonds

▲ Diamonds are forever!

Q1 What does sulphur look like?

Q2 Which acid is sulphur used to make?

Q3 Why is phosphorus stored under water?

Q4 Name the two forms of carbon. Describe their different properties.

1. Metals and non-metals

Heating non-metals

Only a few non-metals are solids. In this experiment you will look at what happens to iodine and sulphur when they are heated. Iodine and sulphur are typical non-metal solids.

Iodine and Sulphur are solids like me – but that's where the similarity ends!

Iodine

A Use a spatula to place *one* iodine crystal into a flask. Put a bung in the top.

B Put a piece of white paper behind your flask. Now warm the flask with your hands.

Sulphur

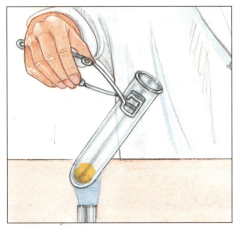

C Your teacher will gently warm some sulphur in a test tube. Once it has melted, the sulphur can be heated more strongly.

D Your teacher will pour the dark liquid into a beaker of cold water.

Apparatus
- iodine
- stoppered flask
- sulphur
- spatula
- white paper
- test tube with holders
- Bunsen burner
- beaker

Safety note: Do not let iodine crystals touch your skin.

Q1 What do you see in step **B**?

Q2 Are there strong or weak forces between the molecules in solid iodine?

Q3 Iodine does not melt. It turns from a solid straight into a gas, without turning into a liquid. How can you separate a mixture of sand and iodine?

Safety note: Your teacher will do this experiment in a fume cupboard.

Q4 Does sulphur have a high or a low melting point? Compare it to your results for iron on page 4.

Q5 What happens in step **D**?

Q6 Which have higher melting points – metals or non-metals?

Extension exercise 2 can be used now.

1. Metals and non-metals

Non-metals: gases

Oxygen, Chlorine, Helium and Neon. These non-metals are a real gas!

Most of the non-metals are **gases**. Room temperature is usually about 20°C. This is well above the boiling point of most non-metals. For example, look at oxygen's melting point and boiling point on this chart:

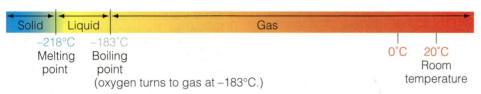

Solid	Liquid	Gas
−218°C Melting point	−183°C Boiling point (oxygen turns to gas at −183°C.)	0°C — 20°C Room temperature

The non-metal gases have very weak forces between their particles.

▲ Helium is very light. It is used inside airships. It does not burn and so it is much safer than hydrogen.

▲ Chlorine is toxic (poisonous). It is dissolved in very small amounts in swimming baths. We use just enough to kill bacteria, without it harming us.

▲ Oxygen is used for welding and in breathing apparatus.

Q1 Why is chlorine added to the water in a swimming pool?

Q2 Look at the start of this newspaper story:

> **Pool of Tears!**
> Fifteen children and four adults were rushed to hospital today from a local swimming baths. The people were having difficulty breathing and had sore eyes.

  a What do you think had happened?
  b Which non-metal gas could be used in the hospital to help the patients breathe more easily?

Q3 Write a list of uses of non-metal gases.

Q4 Chlorine's melting point is −101°C. Its boiling point is −35°C. Draw a chart for chlorine, like the one at the top of this page.

▲ Rockets carry liquid oxygen to burn their fuel in space.

▲ Neon glows red in these signs.

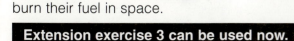

Extension exercise 3 can be used now.

1. Metals and non-metals

Bromine: the non-metal liquid

There are only two elements that are liquids at room temperature. One is that very strange metal, mercury. The other is the non-metal, bromine.

Your teacher will show you an experiment with bromine.

Bromine is a great mixer!

Apparatus
- 2 gas jars
- bromine
- dropper
- fume cupboard

Safety note: Take care near bromine. Its vapour is poisonous. Wear eye protection.

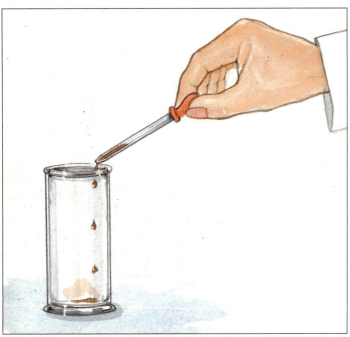

A Your teacher will put a few drops of bromine into a gas jar in the fume cupboard.

B Put another gas jar quickly on top. Leave the jars in the fume cupboard. Look at the experiment every ten minutes.

Diffusion

The bromine molecules easily escape from the liquid. The forces between the molecules are very weak. In fact, bromine boils at just 59°C.

When the bromine molecules evaporate, they mix with the air molecules. Remember that gas molecules zoom around very quickly. They move in any direction and bounce off anything they hit. Eventually, the bromine molecules will be spread evenly throughout the gas jar.

This movement of one substance through another is called **diffusion**.

Q1 What do you see in the gas jars at the end of the experiment?

Q2 Copy and complete these sentences:

Bromine has _____ forces between its molecules. They can easily _____ from the surface of the liquid.

The bromine molecules then d_____ through the air.

Q3 Copy this diagram. Then draw in the particles after diffusion.

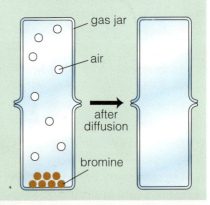

Extension exercise 4 can be used now.

1. Metals and non-metals

Metals v. non-metals

Here is a summary of the properties of metals and non-metals:

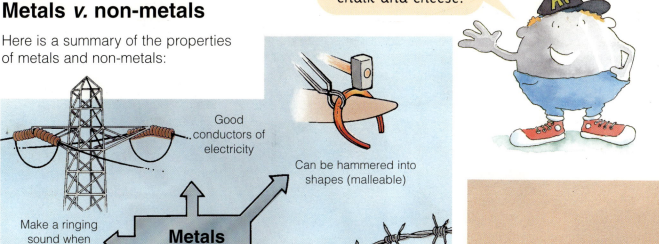

Metals and non-metals – we're like chalk and cheese!

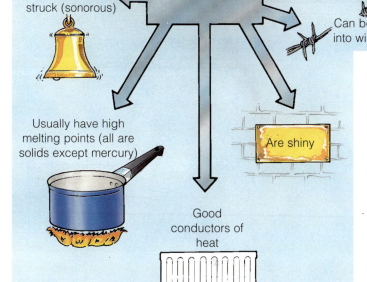

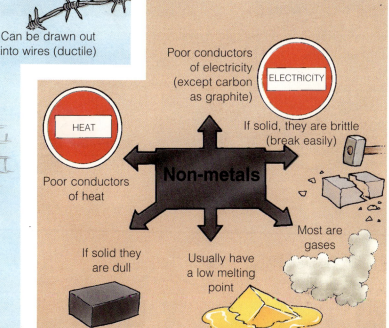

Q1 Copy and complete this table to show the properties of the metals and non-metals. The first one is done for you.

Property	Metal	Non-metal
Shiny	Yes	No

Q2 Look at the three elements, X, Y and Z in this table:

Element	Melting point (°C)	Does it conduct electricity?	Is it shiny?
X	119	no	no
Y	1064	yes	yes
Z	328	yes	yes

Decide whether each element is a metal or non-metal.

Q3 Which is the **best** property to help you decide whether an element is a metal or a non-metal?

Q4 Name any metals and non-metals which have properties that do not fit into the normal pattern. Say why for each one that you have chosen.

Extension exercise 5 can be used now.

1. Metals and non-metals

Making oxygen

 Oxygen is one of my favourite non-metals!

Oxygen is a very important non-metal. It makes up about 20 per cent (one fifth) of the air around us. Most of the rest is nitrogen. Oxygen is the reactive gas in the air. When things burn, they react with oxygen. When living things breathe, they use up oxygen.

In this experiment you can make some pure oxygen gas. Let's use it to find out more about metals and non-metals.

Apparatus

- flask fitted with thistle funnel and delivery tube ■ spatula
- hydrogen peroxide solution (10 volume) ■ trough ■ splint
- manganese (IV) oxide ■ tongs
- Bunsen burner ■ 3 large test tubes with bungs ■ iron wool
- heat-proof mat ■ test tube rack
- magnesium ribbon
- universal indicator solution

Safety note: Wear eye protection.

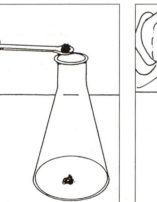

A Put two spatulas of manganese oxide into your flask.

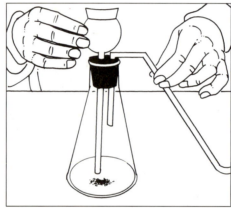

B Add a thistle funnel and delivery tube.

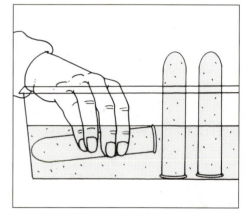

C Half fill a trough with water. Fill three large test tubes with water. Turn them upside down under the water, ready to collect the gas.

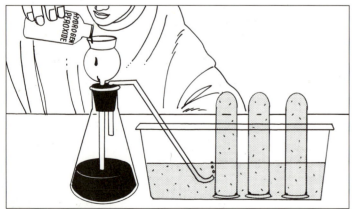

D Place the end of the delivery tube into your trough. Pour hydrogen peroxide down the thistle funnel until you see bubbles coming out in the trough. Let the first few bubbles escape.

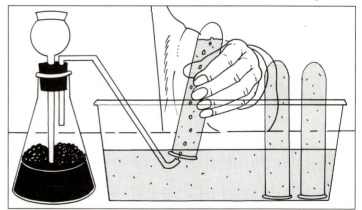

E Now hold one of your large test tubes above the end of the delivery tube to collect the oxygen gas.

F Put a bung into the end of each tube when it is full of gas. Place each test tube into a rack.

1. Metals and non-metals

Testing for oxygen

G Light a splint, then blow it out. While it is still glowing, put it inside one of your test tubes of oxygen. This is the test for oxygen.

Burning metals in oxygen

You can now use your other two test tubes of oxygen gas to burn some metals.

H Hold one end of a piece of magnesium ribbon in a pair of tongs. Use a Bunsen burner to light the other end of the magnesium.

I Put the burning magnesium into one of your tubes of oxygen.

J When the reaction has finished, add a few drops of universal indicator solution to the test tube. Put the bung back in the test tube and shake it.

K Repeat steps **H** and **I** using iron wool.

Safety note:
Wear eye protection. Do not look directly at burning magnesium.

Q1 Copy this diagram which shows how to make oxygen gas.

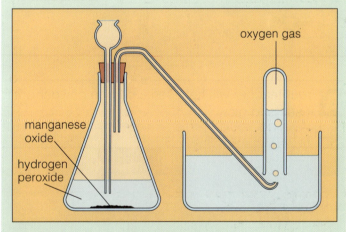

Q2 What is the test for oxygen gas? (Hint: see **G**.)

Q3 What did you see happen in steps **H**, **I** and **K**?

Q4 Elements react with oxygen to make oxides. When magnesium reacts with oxygen, it makes magnesium oxide. We say that the magnesium is **oxidised**. When anything is oxidised, it has oxygen added chemically to it.

Copy and complete this word equation:
magnesium + oxygen ⟶ _____ _____

Q5 In **J**, is the magnesium oxide acidic, alkaline or neutral?

1. Metals and non-metals

Burning non-metals in oxygen

Your teacher will now show you how some non-metals react with oxygen.

Even other non-metals like Oxygen!

Apparatus
- 2 gas jars of oxygen with lids
- carbon powder ■ sulphur powder
- 2 combustion spoons
- universal indicator solution
- Bunsen burner ■ heat-proof mat
- fume cupboard

Safety note:
Sulphur dioxide is a poisonous gas.
Wear eye protection.

A Your teacher will heat some carbon powder until it starts to glow.

B Your teacher will place it inside a gas jar of oxygen gas. When the reaction has ended, quickly slide the lid back on the gas jar.

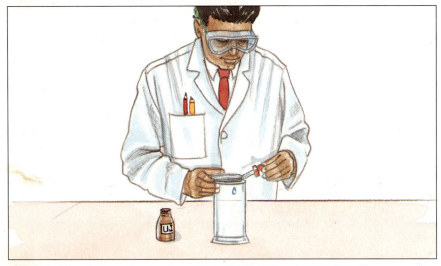

C Add a little universal indicator solution to the gas jar and swirl it round.

D Your teacher will now repeat the experiment, this time burning sulphur. This *must* be done in a fume cupboard.

Q1 What do you see when the following burn in oxygen?
 a carbon
 b sulphur

Q2 With most non-metals, the oxides made are gases. Carbon makes carbon dioxide gas. Sulphur makes sulphur dioxide gas.

Write word equations for both reactions.

Q3 What gets oxidised (has oxygen added to it) in each reaction?

Q4 What happens when universal indicator is added after the reactions? What does this show?

Testing the pH of oxides

In this experiment you can test some oxides which have been dissolved in water. Let's find the pH number of each solution. Remember that the pH tells you how strong or weak an acid or alkali is.

Here is a reminder of the pH scale:

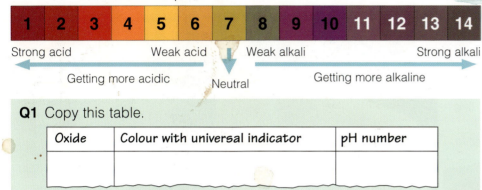

This really is the acid test for metals and non-metals!

Apparatus
- solutions of oxides
- droppers ■ test tubes
- universal indicator solution
- pH chart ■ test tube rack

Safety note: Wear eye protection.

Q1 Copy this table.

Oxide	Colour with universal indicator	pH number

A Put a little oxide solution into a clean test tube.

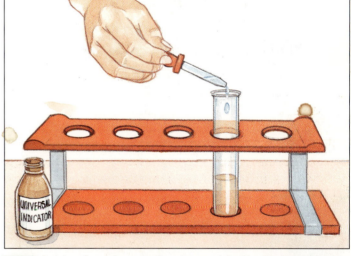

B Add a few drops of universal indicator solution.

C Now match the colour of your solution to a pH scale chart. Complete your table.

D Repeat the experiment with each oxide solution. Make sure you use a clean test tube each time.

Q2 Use your results, and the results on pages 11 and 12, to complete this table:

Alkaline oxides	Acidic oxides

Q3 Copy and complete this rule:
Metal oxides (which dissolve in water) are _____, but non-metal oxides are usually _____.

13

1. Metals and non-metals

Metals, non-metals and the Periodic Table

All the elements are listed in the Periodic Table. The metals are shaded in blue and the non-metals in red. Notice that the dividing line is like a staircase.

Some of the elements near the staircase are not shaded in. These have some properties of metals and some of non-metals. They are called **semi-metals** or **metalloids**.

Look at the picture of the element silicon (Si). Silicon is a semi-metal. It is shiny, like a metal, but is brittle like a non-metal. It does conduct electricity, but not as well as a metal.

Look for me in the Periodic Table. You'll find me under the staircase!

◀ ▲ Silicon is a semi-conductor. It is used in the micro-electronics industry to make transistors and silicon chips.

1	2						Groups				3	4	5	6	7	8
							H									He
Li	Be										B	C	N	O	F	Ne
Na	Mg										Al	Si	P	S	Cl	Ar
K	Ca	Sc	Ti	V	Cr	Mn	Fe	Co	Ni	Cu	Zn	Ga	Ge	As	Se	Br	Kr
Rb	Sr	Y	Zr	Nb	Mo	Tc	Ru	Rh	Pd	Ag	Cd	In	Sn	Sb	Te	I	Xe
Cs	Ba	La	Hf	Ta	W	Re	Os	Ir	Pt	Au	Hg	Tl	Pb	Bi	Po	At	Rn

 metals

 non-metals

☐ semi-metals or metalloids

Q1 Are there more metals or non-metals in the Periodic Table?

Q2 Why are the metals shaded in blue and the non-metals in red?

Q3 What is a semi-metal?

Q4 Do a short research project on silicon. Find out where it is found and what we use it for.

2. The Reactivity Series

Reactivity of metals

This diagram shows you what happens when metals react with acid.

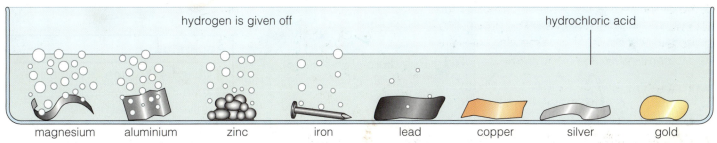

The bubbles of gas are hydrogen.

▲ Iron rusts. It reacts with water and oxygen in the air. Iron loses its shiny surface. It gets **tarnished**.

▲ When iron rusts it is a slow reaction. However, some other metals are so reactive that they must be kept away from the air or water. Metals like lithium, sodium and potassium are stored in oil.

◄ Other metals are so unreactive that they stay shiny for a long time. They do not tarnish. We use these metals, such as gold, to make jewellery.

> **Q1** Look at the diagram at the top of the page. Which of the metals shown is most reactive?
>
> **Q2** What is made when iron is left in air and water?
>
> **Q3** Which gas in the air does iron react with?
>
> **Q4** Why must we store some metals under oil?
>
> **Q5** Why do we use gold to make jewellery?

2. The Reactivity Series

Highly reactive metals

Group 1 is the first column in the Periodic Table. It contains the most reactive metals. They are called the **alkali metals**.

Your teacher will show you how lithium, sodium and potassium react with water.

Li	Lithium
Na	Sodium
K	Potassium
Rb	Rubidium
Cs	Caesium

Watch out for this family of metals! They're really reactive.

Apparatus
- lithium ■ sodium ■ potassium
- knife ■ tile ■ tweezers ■ trough
- universal indicator solution
- paper towel ■ safety screen

Safety note: Wear eye protection during your teacher's demonstration. These metals and their products are flammable and corrosive.

Q1 Copy this table.

Alkali metal	1 What it looks like	2 How hard it is	3 Observations with water
Lithium			
Sodium			
Potassium			

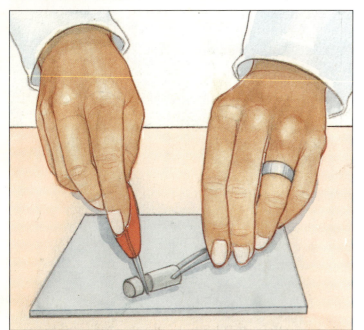

A Watch your teacher cut the alkali metals. Complete columns **1** and **2** of the table.

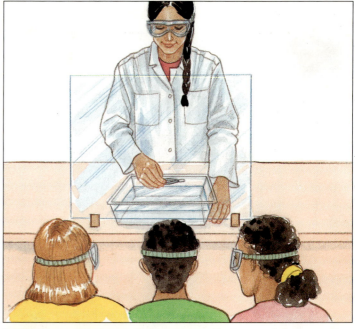

B Your teacher will put a small piece of the metal into a trough of water. Watch carefully.

C When the reaction has stopped, your teacher will add some universal indicator to the trough.

Complete column **3** of your table.

Q2 Why are the alkali metals stored under oil (or paraffin)?

Q3 Which is the hardest alkali metal?

Q4 Put the three metals in order of reactivity (most reactive first).

2. The Reactivity Series

Calcium and water

You have seen some very reactive metals reacting with water. As they react they give off hydrogen gas. In this experiment you can try the reaction yourself, using calcium metal.

It's Top of the Pops – and here's Hydrogen!

Apparatus

- calcium ■ tweezers ■ splint ■ beaker or trough
- test tube ■ universal indicator paper ■ pH chart

Safety note:
Wear eye protection.
Take care not to touch calcium or the solution made in the reaction.

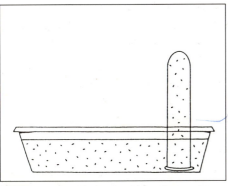

A Put some water in a trough or beaker. Have a test tube full of water upside down in it, ready to catch any gas.

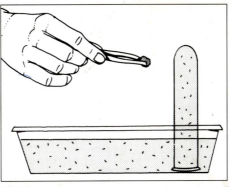

B Use tweezers to drop a piece of calcium into the water.

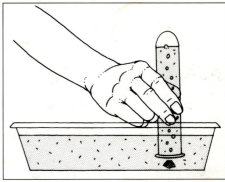

C Collect a test tube full of the gas given off.

D Get a lighted splint ready. Lift your test tube out of the water and test it.

E Use universal indicator paper to test the solution left.

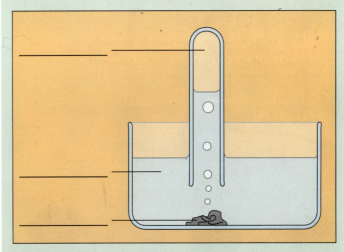

Q1 Copy this diagram and fill in the labels:

Q2 Is calcium more reactive or less reactive than lithium, sodium and potassium?

Q3 What is the gas given off? How did you test for it?

Q4 What happens in step **E**?

Q5 Copy and complete this word equation:
calcium + water ⟶ calcium hydroxide + _____

2. The Reactivity Series

Magnesium and water

Do you remember the alkali metals in water? Potassium reacted faster than sodium. Sodium reacted faster than lithium. We can put them in order of reactivity:

1 potassium
2 sodium
3 lithium

This is the top of a league table called the **Reactivity Series**.

Calcium is fourth in the league.

Your teacher will show you how magnesium reacts with water.

Let's see how my next-door neighbour, Magnesium, gets on with water.

 A Drop a piece of magnesium ribbon into a beaker of water.

Apparatus

- beaker ■ magnesium ribbon ■ boiling tube
- bung with straight tube ■ ceramic wool
- clamp stand ■ Bunsen burner ■ heat-proof mat
- splint ■ safety screen

Safety note:
Wear eye protection during your teacher's demonstration.

Q1 What happens when magnesium is added to cold water?

Q2 Copy this diagram.

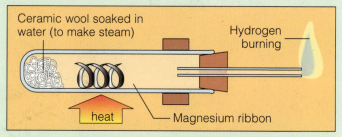

Q3 What do you see when magnesium reacts with steam?

Q4 Where will you put magnesium in the league table?

Q5 Copy and complete this word equation:

magnesium + steam ⟶ magnesium + _____
           (water)   oxide

B Your teacher will now heat some magnesium ribbon in steam. Hydrogen gas is given off in the reaction. The hydrogen can be lit at the end of the delivery tube.

2. The Reactivity Series

Metals in competition

Some metals won't even react with steam. However we can put metals into competition against each other to see which is more reactive. It's a bit like the FA Cup for metals!

Competition reactions

In this experiment, the metals will be 'fighting' over oxygen. The metal oxide has the oxygen to start with. The second metal will try to take it away!

Q1 Copy this table.

Metal and metal oxide	Observations
Iron + copper oxide	

Apparatus
- spatula
- iron filings
- copper oxide
- test tube
- test tube holders
- evaporating dish
- Bunsen burner
- heat-proof mat

Safety note: Wear eye protection.

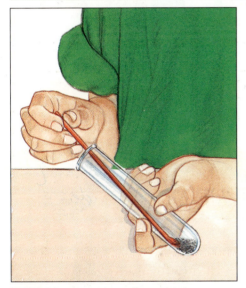

A Mix two spatulas of iron filings with one spatula of copper oxide in a test tube.

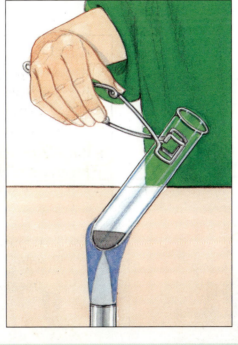

B Heat the mixture strongly for a few minutes. After the tube has glowed red, let it cool down. Empty it into an evaporating dish to see if any copper has been made. Complete your table.

C Your teacher will heat some other mixtures on a tin lid. Complete your table.

Q2 Which pairs reacted in steps **B** and **C**?
If you see a reaction, it means that the metal which started off by itself has 'won its match'. If there is no reaction, the metal which started off with the oxygen has 'won'.

Q3 Write down the 'matches' you saw in steps **B** and **C**. (For example, iron v. copper) Underline the 'winner' each time.

Q4 Now arrange those metals you can in order of reactivity.

Q5 Here are the semi-finals in this year's Metal FA Cup:

Semi-finals	Final
copper v. magnesium	_____
	v. **Cup winners** _____
zinc v. iron	_____

Copy and complete the competition.

2. The Reactivity Series

Displacement reactions

▼ The competitions between metals are called **displacement reactions**. The more reactive ('stronger') metal takes the oxygen away from the less reactive metal. The less reactive ('weaker') metal is left by itself. It is **displaced**.

▼ A less reactive metal cannot displace a more reactive metal.

magnesium + copper oxide ⟶ magnesium oxide + copper

copper + magnesium oxide ⟶̸ no reaction

▼ Here are some other ways we can use to explain displacement reactions.

Q1 Think of other ways to show what happens in displacement reactions.
Draw or explain your ideas.

2. The Reactivity Series

The Reactivity Series

Our league table of metals is called the Reactivity Series. Here is part of the series. It shows the metals we have looked at so far.

Most reactive ↑ ... ↓ Least reactive

Metals (in order)	Reaction with water	Reaction with acid
K – potassium	React with cold water	Explode with acid
Na – sodium		
Li – lithium		
Ca – calcium		Fizz with acid
Mg – magnesium	React with steam	
Al – aluminium		
Zn – zinc		
Fe – iron		
Pb – lead	No reaction with steam	Reacts with warm acid
Cu – copper		No reaction with acid
Ag – silver		
Au – gold		

You can use this Reactivity Series to **predict** (guess) reactions.

Q1 Use the series to see which metal is 'more reactive' (stronger). Who would win these 'tugs of war'?

Q2 Copy and complete these word equations:

magnesium + iron oxide ⟶ _____ + _____

lead + copper oxide ⟶ _____ + _____

Q3 What do you think happens if you heat iron with zinc oxide?

Extension exercise 6 can be used now.

2. The Reactivity Series

Displacement in solution

Metals can also 'battle' with each other when in solution. In this case, the metals will be 'fighting' over the nitrate in solution.

Apparatus
- 2 large test tubes
- zinc strip
- test tube rack
- copper wire
- lead nitrate solution
- silver nitrate solution

Safety note:
Wear eye protection. Lead nitrate solution is poisonous.

A Put some lead nitrate solution into a large test tube.

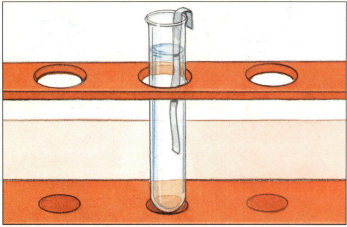

B Fold over the end of a strip of zinc. Hang the zinc in the test tube. Leave it for ten minutes.

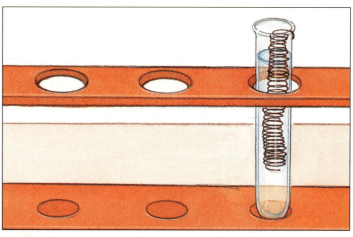

C Set up the same experiment but use silver nitrate solution and copper wire.

Q1 What do you see in step **B**?

Q2 Which metal is more reactive, lead or zinc?

Q3 What do you see in step **C**?

Q4 Which metal is more reactive, silver or copper?

Q5 Copy and complete these word equations:

lead nitrate + zinc ⟶ __*Zinc*__ __*nitrate*__ + _____

silver nitrate + copper ⟶ _____ _____ + _____

2. The Reactivity Series

Predicting reactions

In this experiment you use the Reactivity Series to predict which metals and solutions should react together. Here is an example. Will this reaction happen?

magnesium + copper nitrate ⟶ magnesium nitrate + copper

Magnesium is the more reactive of the two metals, so it should beat copper. Therefore, you would expect to see a reaction.

> **Q1** Copy the table. Predict which will react before starting. Put pencil ticks and crosses in your table.
>
> | Solution \ Metal | Copper | Iron | Magnesium | Zinc |
> |---|---|---|---|---|
> | Copper nitrate | ✗ | | | |
> | Iron nitrate | | ✗ | | |
> | Magnesium nitrate | | | ✗ | |
> | Zinc nitrate | | | | ✗ |

Place your bets! Which metals will win?

Honest Al

✓ = reaction
✗ = no reaction

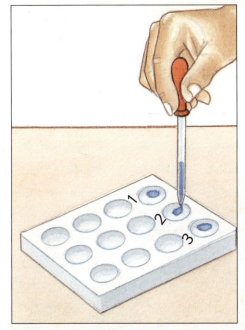

A Use a dropper to put copper nitrate solution into three of the hollows in a spotting tile.

B Use a spatula to add a little iron to **1**, zinc to **2** and magnesium powder to **3**.

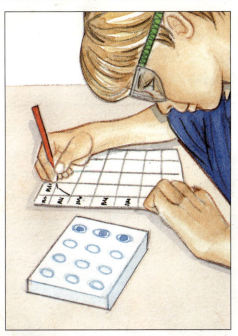

C Look very carefully for any signs of a reaction. Record your results in the table.

D Repeat steps **A**, **B**, and **C** for the other solutions. Complete the table.

Apparatus

- spotting tile ■ spatulas
- solutions of copper nitrate
- iron nitrate ■ zinc nitrate
- magnesium nitrate
- dropping pipettes ■ iron filings
- copper powder ■ zinc powder
- magnesium powder

Safety note: Wear eye protection. Copper nitrate is harmful.

> **Q2** Why does the table in **Q1** start with four crosses already in it?
>
> **Q3** Some reactions are hard to see. Which results were a surprise to you? Check any 'wrong' predictions with your teacher.
>
> **Q4** Choose three ticks from your table. Write word equations for these reactions.

Extension exercise 7 can be used now.

3. Extraction of metals

Metal ores

Most metals are found in Nature as **ores**. Ores are rocks which contain the metal combined with other elements. The metal can be **extracted** from the ore.

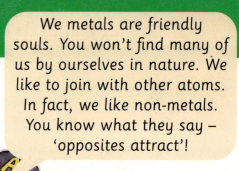

We metals are friendly souls. You won't find many of us by ourselves in nature. We like to join with other atoms. In fact, we like non-metals. You know what they say – 'opposites attract'!

▲ Bauxite is an ore of aluminium. It contains aluminium oxide.

▲ Haematite is an ore of iron. It contains iron (III) oxide.

▲ Malachite is an ore of copper. It contains copper carbonate.

▲ Sphalerite is an ore of zinc. It contains zinc sulphide.

Survey of ores

Your teacher will show you some metal ores.

Q1 Copy and complete this table:

Common name of ore	Chemical name	Metal(s) in ore	Appearance

Q2 What is an 'ore'?

Extracting metals

Gold is one of the few metals found naturally as the metal itself. We say it is found **native**. This is because gold is very unreactive. It would be at the bottom of our league table. (Luckily for gold, metals don't get relegated from the Reactivity Series!)

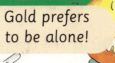

Gold prefers to be alone!

▲ Gold can be found as nuggets!

▲ These miners are searching for gold.

Some other metals can be extracted from their ores by heating them with carbon. Carbon is cheap and there is plenty of it around (coal contains a lot of carbon). Although carbon is a non-metal, we can place it in the Reactivity Series.

K – potassium	
Na – sodium	
Li – lithium	Carbon cannot be used to extract the reactive metals.
Mg – magnesium	
Al – aluminium	
C – carbon	
Zn – zinc	
Fe – iron	
Pb – lead	These metals can be extracted from their ores using carbon.
Cu – copper	
Ag – silver	
Au – gold	

Q1 Why can gold be found in Nature as the metal itself?

Q2 Name four metals that can be extracted from their ores using carbon.

Q3 Many ores are metal oxides. What do you think happens to the carbon when it reacts with the metal oxide?

3. Extraction of metals

Extracting metals with carbon

In this experiment, you can try to extract a metal from its oxide.

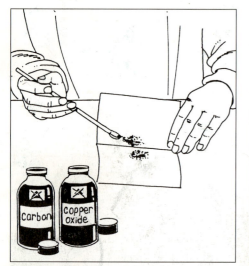

A Fold a piece of scrap paper in two, then open it up again. Collect a spatula of copper oxide and a spatula of carbon powder.

B Thoroughly mix the powders together on the paper.

Apparatus
- piece of scrap paper
- spatula ■ carbon powder
- copper oxide ■ 2 test tubes
- test tube holders
- Bunsen burner ■ heat-proof mat
- lead (II) oxide

Safety note: Wear eye protection. Make sure you don't point your test tube at anyone as you heat it. Do the lead oxide experiment in a fume cupboard.

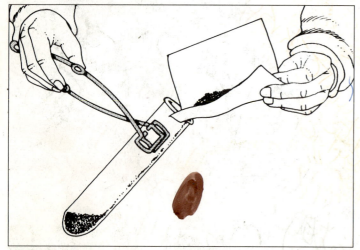

C Slide your mixture into a test tube.

D Heat gently at first, with your test tube at an angle. Make sure it is not pointing at anyone.

E Now heat the test tube strongly for a few minutes. Look for signs of pink copper metal forming inside your test tube.

Do the next part of the experiment in a fume cupboard.

F Repeat steps **A** to **E**, using lead oxide instead of copper oxide.

Q1 Which is more reactive – copper or carbon?

Q2 Describe in your own words how copper was formed.

Q3 Copy and complete this word equation:
copper oxide + _____ → carbon dioxide + _____

Q4 Write the word equation for the extraction of lead from lead oxide.

3. Extraction of metals

The blast furnace

Steel is the most widely used metal in everyday life. Steel contains more than 99% iron. Iron can be extracted from its ore, haematite (iron oxide). The ore is heated with carbon. This is done on a large scale in the **blast furnace**.

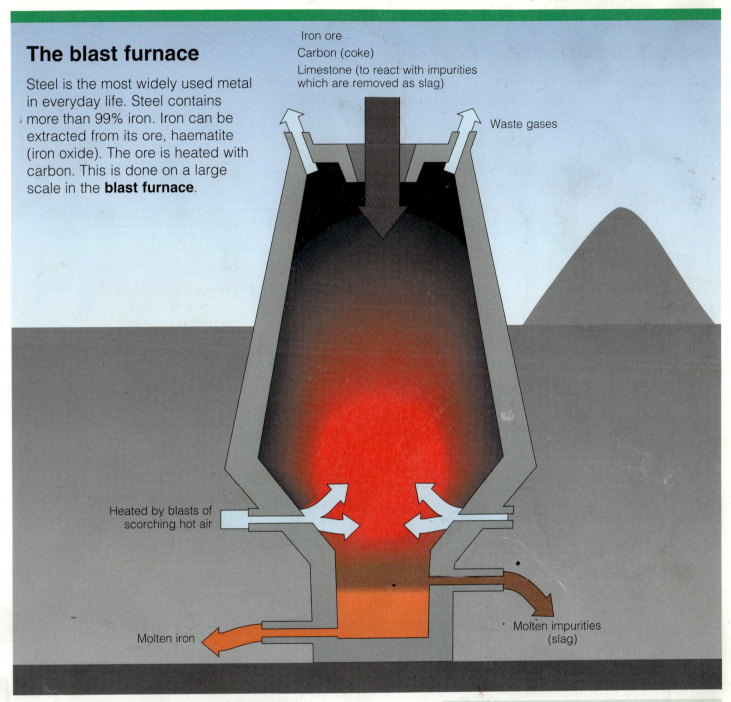

One of the reactions in the blast furnace is:

iron oxide + carbon ⟶ iron + carbon dioxide

The iron oxide has been turned into iron. It has lost its oxygen. We say that the iron oxide has been **reduced**.

At the same time, the carbon has had oxygen added to it. It has been **oxidised**.

Oxidise (adding oxygen) and reduce (taking away oxygen) are chemical opposites.

Q1 What is the ore of iron called?

Q2 Which important metal is iron turned into?

Q3 Explain the words oxidise and reduce.

Q4 Copy the word equation for the reaction in the blast furnace. Which substance has been reduced and which has been oxidised?

Extension exercise 8 can be used now.

3. Extraction of metals

Methods of extraction

The way a metal is extracted from its ore depends upon its reactivity. Carbon cannot be used to extract highly reactive metals. For example,

aluminium oxide + carbon ⟶̸ no reaction

Carbon is not reactive ('strong') enough to take the oxygen from the aluminium. Carbon cannot reduce aluminium oxide.

K – potassium
Na – sodium
Li – lithium
Ca – calcium
Mg – magnesium
Al – aluminium

These reactive metals are extracted by **electrolysis**. Electrolysis means breaking down a substance using electricity. Their ores are melted, then electricity is passed through.

Zn – zinc
Fe – iron
Pb – lead

The ores of these metals can be reduced with carbon.

Cu – copper
Ag – silver
Au – gold

These metals can be found as the metal itself (native).

Q1 What does electrolysis mean?
Q2 Name three metals extracted using electrolysis. What do they have in common?
Q3 Why can't we use carbon to extract aluminium?
Q4 What must be done to a metal ore before electricity can be passed through it?
Q5 Name three metals that can be found in nature as the metal itself. What do these metals have in common?

Extension exercises 9, 10, 11 and 12 can be used now.

4. Thermal decomposition

Heating up and breaking down!

Some substances are broken down when you heat them. This is called **thermal decomposition**. It's a bit like taking a LEGO model apart.

Heating magnesium carbonate

In this experiment you will decompose magnesium carbonate.

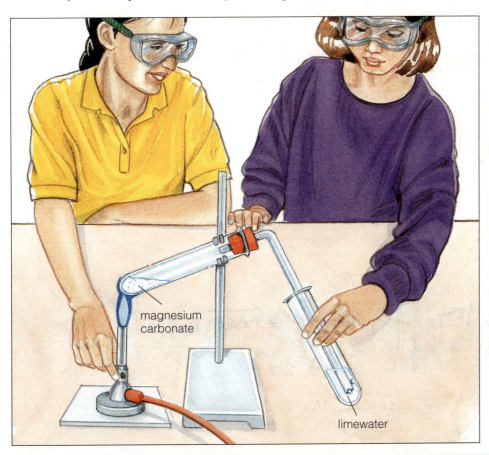

Apparatus
- magnesium carbonate
- spatula   ■ limewater
- large test tube
- bung and delivery tube
- Bunsen burner
- heat-proof mat   ■ clamp stand

Safety note: Wear eye protection. Take care not to let limewater 'suck back' into your hot test tube.

A Set up your apparatus.

B Heat the tube with the magnesium carbonate. Keep heating until you see a change in the limewater. Take the end of the delivery tube from the limewater before you stop heating. This stops cold water being 'sucked back' into the hot tube as it cools down.

Q1 Draw and label this diagram.

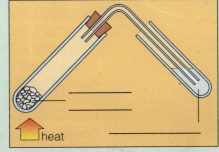

Q2 Which gas is given off?

Q3 Copy and complete this word equation:

magnesium carbonate $\xrightarrow{\text{heat}}$ magnesium oxide + _____ _____

Q4 What do we call this type of reaction?

4. Thermal decomposition

More decomposition

Your teacher will show you some other thermal decomposition reactions.

Apparatus
- potassium manganate (VII) crystals
- clamp and stand
- splint
- lead nitrate crystals
- 2 test tubes
- Bunsen burner
- heat-proof mat
- ceramic wool
- fume cupboard
- safety screen

Safety note: Wear eye protection.

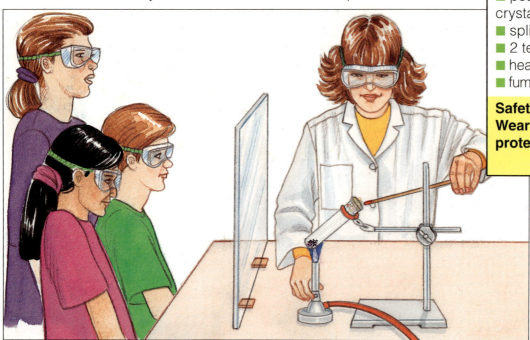

A Watch your teacher heat some potassium manganate (VII) crystals. Test the gas given off with a glowing splint.

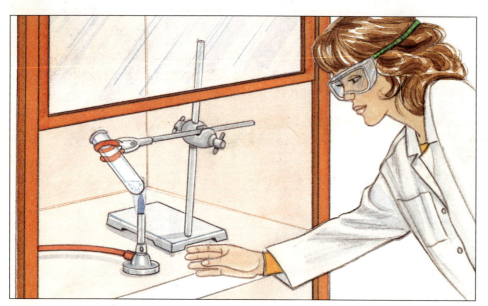

B Watch your teacher heat some lead nitrate crystals in a fume cupboard.

Q1 Which gas is given off when we heat potassium manganate?

Q2 What do you see when lead nitrate is heated?

Q3 What do you think happened to the substances heated in steps A and B?

An investigation

Which carbonate breaks down most quickly?

Apparatus
- copper carbonate
- sodium carbonate
- magnesium carbonate
- selected apparatus
- planning sheet

Use the Planning sheet to plan an investigation to find out which carbonate breaks down most quickly. Hint: page 29 will help you to decide what you need.
How will you tell which breaks down fastest?
How will you make it a fair test?
Show your plan to your teacher before you try it out.

4. Thermal decomposition

Limestone

We use a lot of limestone. It is an important raw material for the building industry. It is also used to make alkalis. The chemical name of limestone is calcium carbonate ($CaCO_3$). Its thermal decomposition is an important reaction in industry.

Reactions with limestone

Apparatus

- piece of limestone ■ tin lid ■ tripod
- Bunsen burner ■ heat-proof mat ■ tweezers
- glass rod ■ 2 $100\,cm^3$ beakers ■ dropper
- filter funnel ■ filter paper ■ $100\,cm^3$ flask
- drinking straw ■ universal indicator solution

**Safety note:
Wear eye protection.**

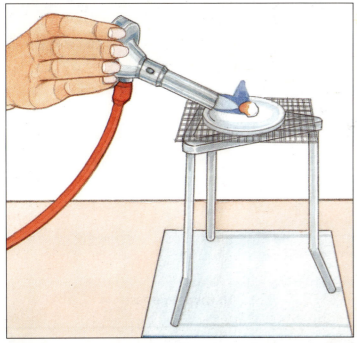

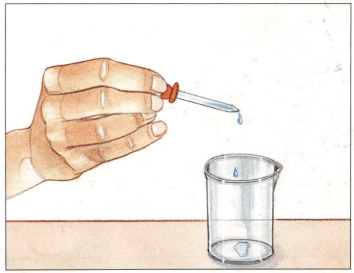

A Heat a piece of limestone strongly. Try to get as much of it to glow as you can.

B Let the solid cool down. Use tweezers to place the limestone into an empty beaker.

C Carefully add a little water from a dropper. Add one drop at a time.

D When there is no more reaction, add $50\,cm^3$ of water to your beaker. Stir it with a glass rod.

E Filter your mixture into a flask.

F Pour about half of your filtered solution into a small beaker. Then gently blow into it through a straw.

G Add a few drops of universal indicator to the filtered solution left in the flask.

Q1 Which step in your experiment involved thermal decomposition?

Q2 Which gas is given off when limestone is broken down? (Hint: see page 29.)

Q3 Name the solution that you made in **E**. Which gas does this solution test for in **F**?

Q4 Is limestone a raw material for making acids or alkalis? (Hint: see **G**.)

31

4. Thermal decomposition

Uses of limestone

We get limestone from huge quarries. Some of it is crushed and used to make roads. Much of the limestone is made into **lime** and **cement**.

The limestone is roasted in lime kilns. This breaks it down into lime (sometimes called quicklime).

Calcium carbonate $\xrightarrow{heat}$ calcium oxide + carbon dioxide
                                    (lime or quicklime)

When heated with clay, limestone gives us cement. Cement mixed with sand, small stones and water makes **concrete**. Concrete is the most widely used material in the building industry.

Here are some uses of limestone and lime:

▲ A limestone quarry.

▲ Many plants don't like acid soil. Farmers neutralise soil with lime.

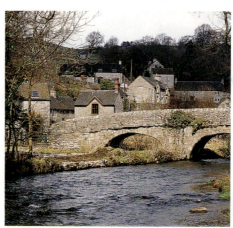
▲ Limestone is used by builders.

▲ Lime or cement, mixed with sand and water, makes mortar.

▲ Concrete was used to make this building.

▲ Limestone is used in the blast furnace to get rid of sandy impurities.

▲ Limestone is also a raw material in making glass.

Q1 Draw a poster showing some uses of limestone.

Q2 A mining company wants to start a new limestone quarry in the Peak District National Park. There are mixed feelings in the area to these plans. Make a list of advantages and disadvantages.